heart strings
by clarice goetz

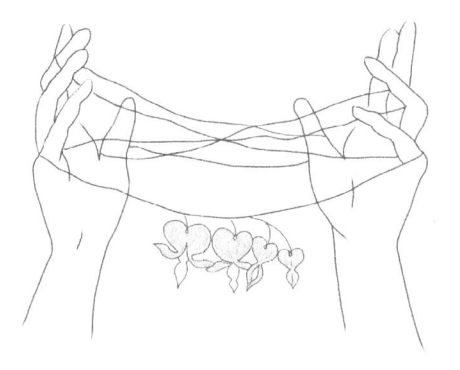

heart strings Copyright © 2020 by Clarice Goetz.
All rights reserved. This book or any portion therof may not be reproduced or used in any manner whatsoever without written permission except for the use of brief quotations in a book review or scholarly journal.

Cover & illustrations by Clarice Goetz.
ISBN-13: 9798567184042

*For my sisters:
Monika, Nicole & Kiersten.*

And to anyone who has heart strings that they wish they could cut. I hope this helps you find the beauty in having the capacity for them in the first place.

foreword

When I was very young, there was a bleeding hearts bush in our garden in the backyard. The image has stuck with me since childhood and evokes deep emotions in me, for people that I have loved and lost in some way or another. The idyllic *Language of Flowers* has taught me many things about flowers and their secret meanings. For thousands of years flowers have been attributed different meanings. Single flowers and arrangements have served as a means of communicating these sentiments, especially when words have failed. It was decided by someone at some point that bleeding hearts symbolize unconditional love.

I have been lucky to love and be loved as deeply as I have in my life. I have also had my heart broken devastatingly more than once. What I've come to understand is that sometimes when you fall out of connection with someone who was important to you, there are still heart strings suspended between the two of you. I've decided that this is a form of unconditional love; the sentiment of wanting happiness for someone who hurt you, and how they remain tethered to you in some way. Some unconditional love burns quietly as time passes.

It could be for a long-lost friend that you drifted apart from. Or the one that got away. Or an estranged parent.

I've listened to my heart strings intently over the years, and they all seem to say the same thing. As I tuck myself in at night, I fold up my heartbreak and crease each of my mistakes like origami cranes. Releasing them out my window along heart string zip lines, I hope that they'll reach each of them somehow.

If you listen you can hear them echoing,

"I still want the best for you."

"Someone I loved once gave me a box full of darkness.
It took me years to understand that this too, was a gift."

— Mary Oliver

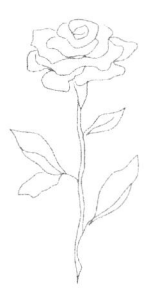

clarice goetz

it was fluttering eyelashes
to morning light
streaming in through sheer curtains.
it was waking to the sight of you;
us smiling in the magic contained in the privilege
of seeing each other first thing.
it was becoming fluent in your breathing.
understanding what all of your sounds meant,
what you needed from me in each shift and stir.
it was stealing kisses and exchanging promises.
it was my cold hands on your warm back.
it was sweaters lent like precious metals,
because your scent was worth more to me
than anything you could have found in a jewelry store.
it was 'I miss you' and 'three more weeks'
and countless voicemails left in the stretches we spent apart.
post stamps and letters,
your blue ink scrawled across lined pages.
it was falling asleep on the phone,
feeling you drift and fade
as our eyes both close
until the line

        drops off on its own.

nothing left now
but a faint dial tone.

heart strings

my love,

I guess this is the end of our journey together.
I hope you know that I don't take one second of it for granted.
it was a privilege to love and grow with you for so long.
I want you to be happy, even if that happiness does not involve me.
I know that it will be hard at first for both of us, but in time,
all the little things that hurt how will fade. but I will
still treasure all of the beautiful memories we shared together.
thank you for being my best friend for so many years.
I love you with all of my heart.
I will miss everything about you.
goodbye.

— C

clarice goetz

breathe him in,
his words are music for those who will listen
catch his eye,
he watches the world with glittering eyes
and waters every neighbour's garden
he grows flowers in my heart
when he smiles at the rain
welcome to my garden

sunflower

heart strings

I don't have all the answers
but I am certain of you
because it has always been you
that gives flight to the butterflies inside me
you who spreads hope like rainfall
and you who pulled me from hiding
with dreams in your eyes.
it has always been you
and the sound of your smile
playing a soundtrack in my sleep.
can you hear all of the words
that I've been aching to say?
that I only go where the lights pull me
and you,
my love,
are the stars.

clarice goetz

when you sing
I'm in a state of reverie
your voice is an invitation to dream
I can't decide if I'm lost
or exactly where I'm meant to be
but from this place
I never want to leave

heart strings

if you die before I do
come back to me as the breeze
please play with my hair
tangle it, I don't care

come back to me as my covers
surround me like water
I imagine that you would
come back to me
in shivers and in warmth

clarice goetz

— my heart feels far away

you took my heart with you
when you left last weekend
you left behind a sweater for me
and forgot your toothpaste
my heart must've got caught on your sleeve
when you kissed me goodbye

you tell me all the things you love about your new town
the friends at your new school
your dorm
the river
the statues on campus
the one that reminds you of us

I want to be where you are now
why do we always fall
at the most inconvenient times?
I want to meet your new friends
I want to go to the theatre
and hold your hand the whole time
feel your smile unfold on my lips
I want to show you how good this can be
I want to be in your city
with you
I want to follow my heart
and find you
right where I left you

— green thumb

all you know
is that you want to paint like your Mom
and garden like your Dad
and have super powers like Matilda
you're anxiously waiting for kindergarten to start
I know you
I know you want to grow up so fast
but the day you get your driver's license
you will drive back to each house you've lived in
and wonder where all the time has gone
where are those matching yellow raincoats
that you and your sisters used to wear?
did they get lost in the last move
or the one before
is the raspberry garden still in the backyard
where are all of the
homemade halloween costumes and paint sets
and endless themed birthdays?
in case you're wondering,
everything will be okay
you and your sisters are still best friends
and yes, your mom taught you how to paint.
you didn't get your dad's green thumb,
but you still love flowers
(and between me and you,
you do have super powers)

clarice goetz

— dad's closet

I remember it so clearly
even though ten years have passed
came home from school,
dropped my backpack
walked toward my father's room
felt the world shift more with every step
I could see from the hallway
that all of his things on his dresser
were gone
drawers and closets had been emptied
checked all of them hoping to be wrong
I pictured him packing up his life
just hours before
I took it in silently as I scanned the room
looking for something he'd worn
I know that I had been naive
but I really didn't think he'd leave
and nothing I could say now
could begin to help myself at fourteen
I sat down in one of the empty closets
and breathed in the scent of him
that lingered still
I don't know how long I sat there
but I never forgot that smell

— **mom**

she was there behind it all
hiding in her own damage,
becoming it.
trying to save her was like
trying to save shadows from the darkness
from where they are whole
and nothing at all.

clarice goetz

don't look at me
like a broken instrument
true, my strings have snapped in places
but they have been restrung
and I can still play the most beautiful music
just like broken crayons
can still colour
I am a symphony
and I will fight hard to play for you

heart strings

       scared doesn't even begin to describe
              my feelings about losing you
                       when I look at you
                       I know that this is it
                         you take my hand
               lead me through this darkness
                the only light I can see is you
              and you say life is meant to be
                             stumbled through

clarice goetz

I tried to capture you
       in a poem –
              but you bled off the
                     edges of every
                            stanza

I tried to capture you
       in a painting –
              but the colours of you
                     mixed together
                            and stained the
                                canvas

I tried to capture you
       in a song –
              but my voice crack-
-ed and the strings snapp-
-ed on all
       of your favourite chords

— **waves**

you fall in and out of love
and take me with you
all of your storms
crashing around me
I have no business spending my time
anywhere that I am not needed

clarice goetz

when I've hurt you
my heart breaks
thinking of all the people
I am failing to be for you

heart strings

I was always sitting right next to you
when I said "I miss you"
and you always replied,
"I'm right here"
but you weren't there
in the place where you miss them
even in the moments where you are right beside them
because you stretched inches
into long distance
and I was chasing what would be
a series of broken promises

clarice goetz

— **passenger**

I don't expect you to follow me
I haven't been pleasant tonight
but I'm tired of carrying the weight of us
and I don't want to be right

I don't want to stay here
I don't like to pretend in real life
but we step inside your front door
like we didn't just have a fight

little paper airplanes crashing
making emergency landings
everything I planned for
up in flames
I'm waiting for relief
always postponing my own peace
until something finds soft ground

— **the anxiety of loss**

clarice goetz

— registrar's office

I sat in the waiting area fidgeting
but I knew that tugging my shirt
would not erase my mistakes
and when I lifted my hands
they trembled
with no one to hold them

heart strings

doesn't matter where I go
what I do
or how old I get
I am the same disappointing self
that I thought I left behind
years ago

— **mental health lies**

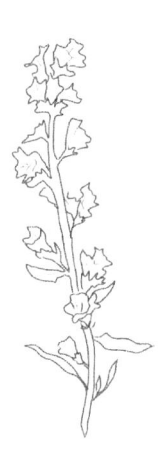

bugloss

clarice goetz

my bones ache from all the lives I am not living
maybe I will always want more
and maybe he will always want less

and less

and less
      and less
    and less

           and less
and le
     ss
        and less

      and less
       and less

                until I am all gone.

if you had a receipt,
would you have taken me back
a long time ago?

        — **exchange or store credit**

— the last call

in the end
it was just a low, defeated,
"is there nothing I can do?"
but his decision was made for us
before I could try
and I sat on the floor surrounded by tissues
holding my stomach like it was hollow
holding my phone to my face
like it was his chest
and listened;
his heart beat distantly
for dreams that no longer involved me
as I lost him in the sound waves

heart strings

when he tried to leave
I pulled out a letter
that he wrote to me two months before
promising a future
and children
who would've had two storytellers for parents
as if presenting this piece of evidence
could have erased that moment's truth
I made him read it in silence
and tortured him for answers
I saw his face crumble in defeat
I remember watching him tug at his fingers
struggling to explain
his departure
but he didn't say a thing
I was headstrong for a moment
demanding the explanation I deserved
but those eyes
will always be the death of me
I couldn't watch him fall apart
so I pulled him into my arms
and released him
from a future he could no longer promise

clarice goetz

we kissed one last time
sweet, even in goodbye
and everything afterwards
tasted pretty sour in comparison
your lips were a promise for someday

I hoped

heart strings

something happens
in the first few blinks
of waking
dreams vanish
they fall off of your eyelashes
and into the dust of the air
I like the look
I used to see in your eyes
in those first few moments
as you tried desperately
and so sweetly
to grasp onto something
that you thought was real
the final time I saw that look
on your face
it was much harder to watch

clarice goetz

— scraps of you

he walked into my heart at sixteen
like it was a party thrown just for him
and even after he left
I never stopped celebrating

my heart aches like he still belongs
but just left the party early
a part of me knows
he won't be making another appearance

the party feels more like a funeral now
there's crumpled streamers on the floor
the lights have all gone down

I shred myself into confetti for him
as I sit here thinking
I would love the scraps of you

heart strings

I lost a person and gained a city
like a little moth in summer heat
drawn to the city lights
I found home in a skyline
and fell in love with my bedroom window;
the way it all lights up at night,
the peach sunrises that kiss my shoulders
and wake me up each morning
my new streets felt like a promise
and I needed something to hold me

it's tricky business
falling in love with a city
I've learned that if you're a moth
flying close to the lights
you have to be prepared
to burn your wings

— aftermath

it's almost harder
when there are no words left to be said
living in the sigh of defeat
that comes after a long struggle
wanting to reach out
to touch
or to be in touch
but having no reason
and no where to hide your longing
but within

heart strings

it all rushes back and forth in your head
all the years spent in love,
growing and learning
until he felt like he had nothing left
to learn from me

you've made a mess out of me

clarice goetz

at the end of the day
when I am alone again
and my world has gone quiet
my phone begs me to call you
out of habit
and I toss for hours
suppressing the impulse
choking on the words
I want to whisper to you
biting my tongue so hard
that tears roll into my ears
pretending I don't want to hear
about your day

— night time routine

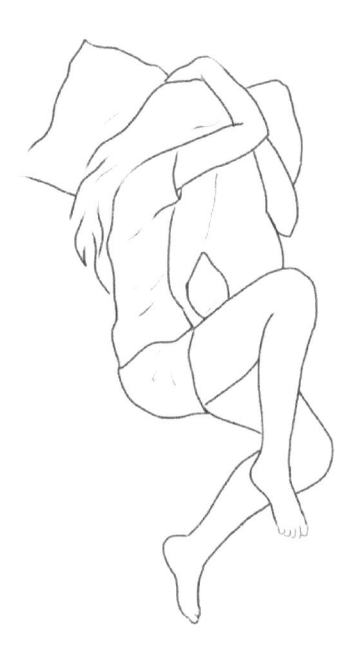

— in the silence

I fought so hard for us
but it was a losing game
why is it always me who surrenders first
you will never be the one to cave
I will live in your silence
for years
watching photographs develop on screens
your face will change
and you will grow
until they're all just images
of a person I don't know

clarice goetz

— finding home

I used to think home was a house
until mine was shaken upside down and emptied
I used to think home was a family
until mine broke and scattered
I used to think home was a person
until my favourite one left

heart strings

can we go back to the garden
or to the forget-me-not beds where we played
can I find a small Kiersten somewhere
running around like a little toad
that's what we called her, once upon a time
Nicole wants to go to the park
I'll hold her hand the whole way there
can I play video games with you, Monika?
we'll pretend to be asleep when Dad comes in

what about our house
our home where everything had a place
suddenly nothing did
suddenly boxes
cutting our losses
suddenly growing up
a lot faster than we expected

photo albums, feeling distant
home videos flickering
I forgot we used to laugh that loudly

what happened in those years
it's all a blur, but we're still here
can we go back, I think I lost myself
I don't know who I was back then
can we please go back
to before all the hurtful things I said

clarice goetz

whenever I am hurting
something about flowers
tends to soothe
I remember sitting
in beds of forget me nots
in my youth
picking dandelions
alongside soccer fields
where later roses grew
I must've learned it from my grandmother
she keeps flower pots on her windowsill
they dance on her china and her bedspread too
she passed down
her heart to me
along with
her floral tendencies

heart strings

when my grandpa wakes up
he makes her breakfast first
carefully counting fruits and nuts
cutting up banana slices
and pouring her cereal
readying her paper towel napkin
for when she wakes
his hands, wrinkled
and cramped from arthritis
his walk stifled by cancer
he keeps track of the things
the doctor wants her to eat
he tells me exactly the portions
she needs each day
as though he were giving me
a recipe for love

clarice goetz

this city
I used to call home
makes me feel like a visitor
driving past my old streets
suburban daydream
looking up,
only power lines and sky
a quarter life of memories
there's nothing here for me now

heart strings

you said
you feel suffocated
by me

and I'm
finding it hard to breathe
without you

this is how it feels
to be too much
and not enough
all at once

clarice goetz

I've been rummaging through our debris
going through the motions
trying to make sense of things

sometimes I find you in everything
my heart recognizes you
even if I don't want to see

some days I find clarity
some days I only find damage in me
who am I now, who were we

heart strings

it was almost cinematic
summer sun on the dash
radio playing a new favourite
I watched you sing
from the passenger side
how surreal
to feel bliss
and ease with you
in the wake of goodbye
speeding down the highway
towards our final moments in a driveway
all of the familiar signs
we've been watching from the backseat
all of our lives
wave goodbye

clarice goetz

you called yourself a coward
when at first
you couldn't bring yourself to leave
I winced
because I think that it is brave
to stay
and fight
I associate cowardice with giving up
I will never understand
why you would be disappointed in yourself
for staying by my side
I was a weakness in your eyes
and all I wanted was to be your strength

— **expectations**

I am in the business
of breaking my own heart
because I expect to get
what I give
and I give everything
for love

— **deflecting**

whenever your name is spoken
I always put the blame elsewhere
for the pain in my chest
you're the one who left, after all
but maybe I am to blame
when all is said and done
maybe you just got tired
or bearing the weight of my mind
for so many years
I wonder how many days I ended with
'I just want to hear your voice'
I wonder how many more are left

peony

heart strings

I think I dreamt of you last night
there were fragments at least
I wonder if I still make appearances in yours
or if I've blown away
in some unceremonious breeze

clarice goetz

a week after
you said you were afraid to sing
because you were scared to lose control
my heart broke again
watching you run from the flood
running from something
we used to share
I hope you found a playlist
that sounds like you
I hope you let it heal
what broke between us
we all deserve to sing
even if it's through tears
I hope you found
the music in you again
I hope you find someone
to sing your harmonies

heart strings

maybe the reason
your tears made me feel closest to you
is because I hardly ever felt them fall
you held so much inside
your spine was always so upright
you were so strong that
at times I forgot
you hurt too.
you pressed all of your feelings
like a flower press
dried out the deepest
parts of yourself
what has become of my garden
only wilting is left

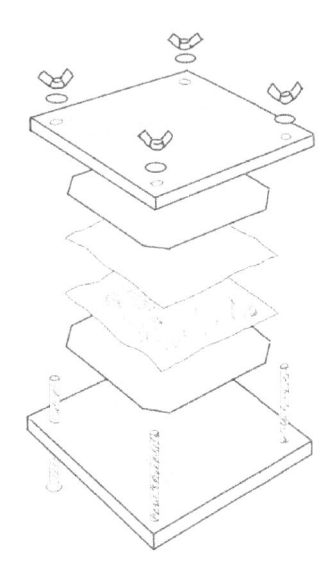

clarice goetz

some days
I feel like myself
and then some days
I turn into no one at all
a person I don't understand
there's me
and there's my shadow
and on the days
when I am a silhouette
I am grateful
for the people who are willing
to recolour me
because they know
that I am capable
of more than grayscale

heart strings

I've been running you through my head
like paper to a shredder
reducing everything
trying to see if I missed something
I've been running scenarios
preparing for the day
that I run into you
bracing myself
for the girl on your arm

clarice goetz

you curse your curves and edges
the ones I held and loved
the ones you deemed unlovable
I have missed every inch of you

heart strings

we're living in the worst time
to be forced apart from someone
because it's so easy to reach for him
in places he won't know I visited

the codes he sends on social media
hit me like bullets
that he didn't know were ammunition

but you can't blame anyone for your pain
if you subscribe to it

— unfollow your ex

— talking walls

I asked if I was the problem
but neither of us was to blame
I was the passionate, impractical one
colouring outside the lines
loving too vividly
suddenly he could picture
his life without me
I faded out of focus
"was I too much?"
I asked my walls
"there is nothing wrong
with the way you love"
they replied
"you weren't asking too much,
you were asking the wrong person"
he was searching for answers
in the wrong eyes;
he needed a mirror

heart strings

all of the sweet nothings
echoing off the walls
like empty prophecies
mocking me

clarice goetz

at night time
I dream of you
in the moments before sleep
your laugh echoes in my ears
like our late night phone calls used to
I'm just waiting for the day
you come home to my arms
I would welcome you in
with warmth and love
all of the familiar things
rushing back into your chest
am I cold on your pillow now
you must think I've closed the door
and locked off my heart
have you checked your pockets lately?
I slipped you a key

heart strings

when there's nothing left to say
when there's no excuse for us to stay
in the space where we hesitate
to give anything more

that's where I'll be,
if you need me.

clarice goetz

when did it begin?
did you wake up one day
and realize
that you would have to be the one to leave
for this to end?
did it hit you too late
had you made too many promises
that you found you couldn't keep?
is that why when I asked
where this was coming from
the words never left your lips?
did it surprise you too?

    — **speechless**

heart strings

even in my wildest fantasies
we still don't end up together
no matter how hard my brain
tries to force the pieces
we still find ourselves in tears
mourning what could have been
my mind is too sharp
for my foolish mind games
even my hypothetical heart
won't bet on us

clarice goetz

— **compromise**

we were so busy
dreaming of someday
that we forgot
to live for now
we were careless
we let ourselves bend
so much that
we lost each other
we thought that
our good days
were still ahead
they're all behind us now

colchicum

heart strings

I leave this place behind
salty-eyed and breathless
our love will stay even if we cannot

— deadlines

why do I feel like I was wiser 4 years ago?
why did the first heartbreak
bring so much good to my soul
but this one just ruined me,
spat out poetry,
and shackled me to the idea
that he was the only one for me?
I thought I was beyond this.
why am I not wiser at 23?

how long did it take last time
to forget the patterns in his eyes?
to stop worshipping his footsteps
as he walks further and further away from me.
to remember that I'm not alone,
if I have myself.

how long
before I recovered
from the shattering?
it's been months
and I'm still finding pieces of glass inside.

it's in the little things
emptying picture frames
returning belongings
the stomach ache
lack of hunger and sleep
text messages typed and backspaced
tears staining my pillowcase
it all comes back
months later
sitting on my bed
cleaning out my voicemail box
getting caught off guard
finding that his voice is still there
places
I thought I'd erased him from

     — **relapse**

clarice goetz

can't reach you the way I used to
extend myself past my welcome
stretch the moments we had
into years spent without you
my whole life
filled with empty promises
always falling short
or far behind
missing arms in the dark
waiting for my heart to restart
when will this life
ever feel like mine

heart strings

the idea of speaking to you
once excited me,
when I was wanted
and the soil of our love was fertile;
oh how we bloomed.
now I think of the rejection
I would face
if I said even a single word to you.
the shame you would cast,
the wilting I would feel inside.
all the rules you play by;
the mature practicality of
distance and silence.
those words just sound like
synonyms of torture to me.

clarice goetz

— **inevitable**

like turning your back to the waves
and closing your eyes;
you know it's coming
but you don't know when or how hard.
I don't think I'll ever be ready
to hear another person's name
on your tongue

heart strings

the year is over now

but did you keep using
that moleskine planner I gave you?

the one embossed with my initials?

did you throw it away?

did it

       hurt?

clarice goetz

I think that
everything that I have done
every move that I have made
every book I have read
every concert I have seen
every night I have felt alone and empty
every single word **I** have written
even the doodles in the margins
has been *because of*
the *aftermath to*
and the *healing from*
what **broke**
between **us**

heart strings

another night
city lights
dance on my wall
lying awake
counting mistakes
thinking him over, tears fall
and he doesn't care about them
not anymore
sheets on skin
he doesn't wish he was holding
why, when it rains
does it pour

clarice goetz

I give into thoughts of you
it is a choice
to let you leak into my daydreams
I helplessly indulge

periwinkle, white

I'm always a breath
away from you
too late or too early
but never on time
the time is never right
I've given you
the best of myself
but our almost
will never be enough

— **timing**

clarice goetz

no one ever talks about
the heartbreak
between two people
who still love each other
I didn't think it could exist
nothing prepared me
for that kind of defeat

heart strings

do you ever feel this rough?
this punch to the gut?
I stumbled in drunk
and crawled into your shirt
dug it out of my closet
like I wanted to hurt
maybe because it's better
than you being gone
completely

— if I saw you

I sometimes imagine what I would do
if I saw you again.
would I act like I was over it?
that I was happier now, without you
with a sharpness in my content

I could play the victim
stare at you with my deepest blue eyes
drown you in guilt for the hurt you caused
make your heart beat for me again,
once more

would I hug you?
in reassurance and forgiveness?
would I keep my distance
as though your skin
would hurt me if I touched it?

in this exact moment,
I do not know
where I'd find the strength to pretend.
I do not think
I'd have the strength
to refuse you

heart strings

you were a home
that I had to leave once,
but never wanted to
your heart didn't belong to me anymore
feeling betrayed,
I left the walls bare and dull
I took everything I owned
and vacated
I should be happy
that someone else moved in
I am the one who left, after all
so why am I lying here
wondering how she decorated?
what colours did she paint you with?
did she fill the rooms that I left empty?
what of the renovations?
did she repair what I neglected?

clarice goetz

if love was enough
we'd be laughing
but there is something to be said
for being alone
for distance
and growth
love just doesn't cut it sometimes
god, I wish it could've

heart strings

there are days I can't help
but think of how it used to be
I can't be blamed for looking back
on the kind of love
who made me flower crowns on dog walks
who left me voicemails during the day,
and called again later for midnight talks
who almost jumped into a river to catch a floating lantern for me
I will start forgetting tomorrow,
I promise.

softly, softly

clarice goetz

I've befriended the heartache
we chat and play cards
like old friends rekindling
my heartache is compassionate
and beautiful in her ruin
she leaves tissues on my nightstand
and helps me write when I can't sleep
she doesn't mind it
when I don't leave my apartment for days
although we do disagree on some things
she thinks she has all the answers
she says that everything I need to know
was explained by the way he left
and that's it. it's done.
but I'm a hopeless romantic
a dreamer
a second
and third chance-giver
and apparently,
not very good at cards

heart strings

"I hope we can be friends someday"
is a seven-word lie
that I say to ease your guilt
once you've kissed the stars
it's impossible to settle for mere stargazing
I've been a student of your astronomy for many years
and I've always wanted more from you
you should know that by now

clarice goetz

I stood in a room full of people
I hadn't seen in years
they always knew me as yours
I think they saw you in my face
did they recognize your name
on my lips?
could they detect the hurt
in my chest?
did the dim lighting hide the salt stains
from tears that ran down my cheeks for you?
I tried to wash it all away
but my body is stained with you
like watercolour

heart strings

I have lived through much worse,
on paper.
I will survive this, too.
on paper.
I will write my way through it.

clarice goetz

I stretch myself at parties
the same way I do in love
holding myself responsible
for someone else's happiness
giving myself away piece by piece
to appease yet another heart

is everyone having a good time?
are you happy?

I host apologetically
making my rounds
stretched paper thin
with no concern for myself
hanging streamers between us
until they fall down
because everyone has left

did everyone have fun?
could I have done something to save us?

heart strings

as you apologize for the inconvenience
I excused you as I hear
another bone break inside my body
from bending to your preferences
for too many years

        — **pretzel**

clarice goetz

realizing that
I am no longer a priority
is a keen sting
that I still haven't gotten used to
how is it so easy for you
to be so cold to me
when you're the one who left?
it's not fair that I still soften
just to bring you ease
and you never offer the same courtesy

the patterns of my mind
travel back to you by default
it works in extremes
in anger or in grief
and all I want to do
is tell you everything
you are always the first person
who comes to mind

clarice goetz

I wonder who you think I am now
what do you see
I'm getting lonely on someone else's arm now
I'm dragging my feet to work
barely faking it enough
to fool my friends

you let my texts slip between your fingers
like little pieces of litter
that you drop when no one's looking
your replies don't phase me now
there was a version of me
that was desperate for any scrap of communication
she would have left any building
dropped any shitty job
to read a single message from you
she was hopeful for us
and I am not

I suppose
there is some victory
in defeat
I don't believe in us anymore

heart strings

you've silenced the parts of you
that sound like me
you call it a void
the ashes of us

mine is less like a void
and more like an admittedly open wound
you might as well be a soundtrack
I never stopped listening

clarice goetz

if I could just make it through one day
without thinking of you,
well, that would be progress.
I went a few hours once
I was busy
the day was moving fast around me
blurring my mind of its usual habits
then quiet fell and I found you again
dancing through my mind,
like the place was yours.
I stood in my mirror, remembering it all
I don't remember the last time
someone kissed my cheek
maybe those were always yours

   — **choreography**

— **cyclical**

who are you to be angry at yourself
for having a heart
big enough to love someone
who left you heartbroken
and blindsided.
forgive yourself
for the love that you've given away freely,
whether they deserved it or not.
don't scold your open heart
the love you give away
comes back to you
always
if you let it;
I promise

— on your birthday

I'm up when the clock turns midnight
it's 12:09 and I'm wondering who you're with
I would've called you around now
this time last year
I hope your phone isn't quiet

12:14, I would've mailed you something surely
a handmade card, always a handmade card
I wonder who's singing to you tonight
is it selfish to send a message
do I have anything to lose
if I've already lost you

12:37, things that used to ring sweet in my ears
have echoed into silence
the last thing you told me
was to please take care of myself
I've never heard anything sound so sad.
except maybe "happy birthday,
from someone you used to love"

— the first year

christmas came and went
after our anniversary
our birthdays passed
and valentine's too
I'm waiting for the first year
to go by without you
replace this reminiscence
with new memories
why do I always make time
to hurt over these things?
I find corners to hide in
to mourn
on what should be the happiest days
why do I always make space for you
when all you wanted was space from me

— **heart strings**

I should probably go
you asked to catch up and we did just that
now I'm hanging from heart strings
that I'm afraid to cut
you're giving me knots in my stomach
I'm impatient and you know it
I have to go before you do
I can't watch you
leave me again

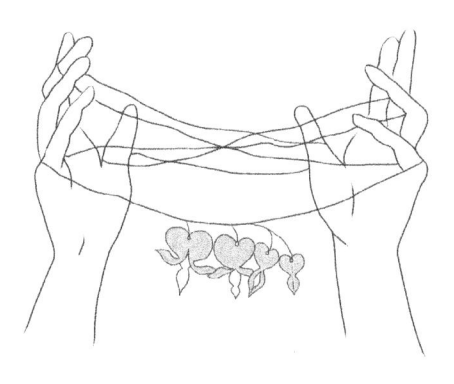

— who to save

why did I decide
that his actions after the fact
were a reflection on me
how could I hold myself accountable
for his silence

I thought love was self-sacrificing
that it meant giving yourself
I was wrong

love is knowing who to save
when someone breaks you
instead of holding you
like they promised to

clarice goetz

I saw us exactly how I wanted to
despite every hint you gave me
that you were not invested
I skim through the evidence now
all the evading I did not see
it was there all along
I was blind because I wanted to be

heart strings

I hate thinking of you alone
because if you were drowning
I know you wouldn't reach for me
you deserve to never be lonely
but I deserve to have someone
who is sure of me

clarice goetz

— elephant

I feel myself start to let go of things
and then panic
when I can't remember little details
I don't want to forget
someone who meant so much to me
why it matters, I can't say
but I am scared that one day
I will wake up
and forget your middle name

I guess I am the only one
holding myself back
from forgetting

heart strings

I have chosen you
again and again
even when you weren't an option

clarice goetz

— with and without

even now
as I sink
no regrets poison my heart
I miss a lot of things
but if I never had you
I know I would've missed more

heart strings

the second hardest part
is saying goodbye
to the life you dreamed up in your head

the hardest part
is letting go of
your best friend

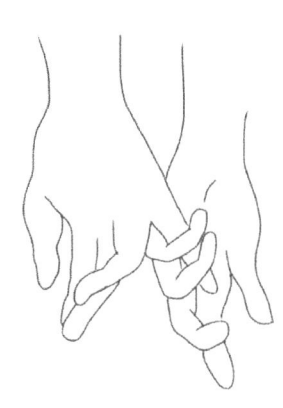

how are you? how's Toronto?

        it's (far enough from my hometown that I feel like I'm carving out my own home, but close enough that I can still hop on a train to share in holidays and birthday cakes. it's a kinetic city, full of static energy. the problem is, sometimes it can shock you. and at times I feel left out because there's all this electricity and yet somehow I'm still longing for a spark. the people here are scrappy. I forgot my manners on public transit a few months ago. they're probably rotting in a lost & found in some subway station in the east end. around the same time, I learned how most people in my area take their coffee) **great!**
I'm busy (overworking myself, hustling at multiple jobs to support a career that at best feels like absolute euphoria and at worst, a toxic one-sided relationship) **but** (I wouldn't have it any other way) **good!**

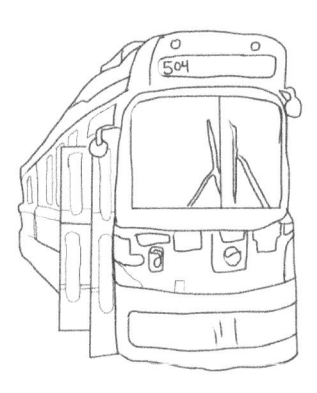

heart strings

                                    mornings and I
                                have always been at war
                                to hunger for life and sunlight
                                 but struggle to rise to it
                              to hesitate to chase my dreams;
                                    this is my battle.
                                     I want to rise
                                     and shine too
                                     to choose life
                          even when it's unimaginably hard
                                 to never opt out of it
                                      I imagine
                                   that life at best
                              is waking up an hour earlier
                              just to live an hour more

clarice goetz

he was last seen driving through
a rolling suburb
one hand relaxed on the steering wheel
eyes kind, like his father's
humming and singing along absentmindedly
the same way you do when you're cooking

he was last seen walking through
a forest of guitars
fingers outstretched and searching
for the answers I could not give him
could I still find you somewhere?
in a studio, barefoot and playful.
in the imaginary apartment we dreamt of sharing, making us afternoon coffee.
or in a movie theatre that only plays your childhood videos
and no one hushes you when you talk through them.

he was last seen in an elevator
pushing the "close door" button repeatedly
annoyed that it stopped on a floor
he never asked for
I wonder how long it took
for the doors to close

heart strings

when I first moved to the city
with my grassy knees
and suburban sparkle
I was so confused
by the blank stares
and jaded, tired faces on the subway.

now mine matches all of theirs.

   — **how to lose colour**

clarice goetz

I miss the layers of me
that love seems to grow
the velvet collarbone kisses
the flirt in my voice on the phone
the joy of buying stamps to send letters
the delicate words that pour out of my pen
the way my heart unfolds like rose petals
when I begin to trust again
I miss the girl who smiles
with ease and certainty
I miss how she glows
I find her here and there
in the mirror
she's still wearing his clothes

heart strings

can you imagine if the people we loved
formed tattoos on our skin?
appearing without warning?
patterns and imprints
telling the story of our hearts
on our skin for all to see
like a map of love and loss
of hurt and life
what would my tattoos look like?
I wonder if people who meet me now
can detect the imprints you left behind.
if our stories coloured my skin
with their imperfect designs,
I would still wear them proudly.

clarice goetz

— back to myself

been coming back to myself lately
coming home to self love instead of my mess
been taking myself out on walks lately
decided I deserve to like how I dress
been listening to the music of my mind lately
realized anyone would be lucky to sing along

heart strings

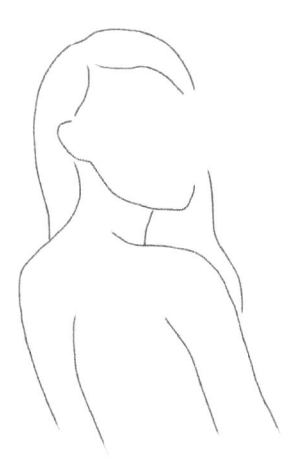

november came
and everything changed
the sky gave me permission to smile
and my heart took on a new life of its own
caught a woman singing in the mirror
and for the first time in months
I recognized her

clarice goetz

— **connect the dots**

you once referred to me
as a masterpiece
a work of art
I'm connecting the dots
that you drew for me
I'm starting to
see it now

heart strings

I am in debt to myself
I owe myself
all the love that I give away
to other people instead

clarice goetz

— self portrait

home is not a house
it's not a family
or another person
home is within you
it's in all the songs you love to sing
when you're home alone
it's in the colours that speak to you
all of your favourite flavours
the way you walk
it's in your handwriting
the books you pick off the shelf
everything you do is your signature
you are home
you were home all along

heart strings

here's to texts from friends
that leave me smiling for days
here's to reading books that make me forget
how tired my heart is
here's to taking myself on dates
and finding myself delightful.
here's to listening to myself by staying in
to watch my favourite show in bed (again)
here's to reminding myself
that I'm doing so much better
than I ever give myself credit for
here's to looking at my reflection
in my window at dusk
layered over city lights
smiling at the thought of how five years ago
I was dreaming about the part of life
I'm living in now

clarice goetz

maybe when two souls
are intertwined for too long
they stay tethered in some way
some nights I wake up
because I can feel him tossing
from miles away
he could be hurting over something
that doesn't concern me
but it tugs at me
like the moon controls the tides
so I wait for him to settle
before I close my eyes
and whisper to the stardust
that lives in both of us
'we will both find our own way'

— the loving part

it's easy to feel like your time was wasted
when everything falls apart
love is never, ever a waste though
it's the loving part
that makes you who you are

clarice goetz

it's not the one you're losing sleep over
or the one who has you questioning your worth
it's not the one you spill tears for
or the one who doesn't return your texts
it's not the one you thought.
no matter how perfect it felt
or how wonderful you think they are
if they were your soulmate, they'd still be here.
if it was really them
you wouldn't be twisted up like this.
love doesn't look anything like
the person your heart carved out for you
but don't worry
when they get here you'll recognize them
as if pieces of you already belonged to each other
you'll come to know them
as the one who will never leave your side
your questions will fall silent
the self-doubt will crumble and fade
and once again
you will learn to redefine love's face.

— dating advice for my future child

you'll know it's right
when they choose you
just as confidently as you choose them
let everyone else fall through the cracks
they were never yours
and you were never theirs
just two souls passing by
on their way to becoming
who they're really meant to be

clarice goetz

I want to be angry for the hurt
I want to be cold
but all I have is softness for you
melting is all I was meant to do
in your presence

— smudges

don't erase the traces of us
don't look back with an empty heart
do you remember the way the leaves fell for us
as we arrived at the cottage last fall?
do you remember the magic?
the sweaters, kisses, notes and voicemails.
remember us this way.
so what, if it wasn't meant to be?
it was meant to be for then.
don't smudge the ink
of the love we printed so boldly.

clarice goetz

you are most beautiful
when you are honest
everyone has a chapter
they don't like to read aloud
but there are hearts out there
that need to hear from yours today

heart strings

grateful for the seeds
I planted in my heart last time
I don't need to wait for flowers
I grew them for myself

clarice goetz

you're the book I never read
but bought into a long time ago.
your inside cover is scrawled with inscriptions
from other promising women
who picked you up
and re-gifted you
or shelved you for something better
some of them ripped out pages
taking pieces of you
that I've been looking for

heart strings

we came alive at night
like constellations
invisible to one another during daylight,
luminant in each other's skies otherwise.
you only light up my phone at night
like an afterthought
or a midnight rush for something you call love
I'll never be the girl you want
to spend Sunday afternoon with.

clarice goetz

I cannot define the word love
without thinking of you first
and I wonder what that means
all the time

— relacing

it ended and it was not because we failed.
I looked in the mirror during our descent
and did not recognize the love I was wearing
my tired eyes and knotted stomach
were not nearly as full as they used to be

it ended and it was not because we didn't try.
it is hard to have greyhound tickets
long distance calling
and 'see you in six weeks'
as normalcy
to build a love almost entirely out of words
I tried. we both tried.

it ended and it was not because we weren't a good match.
it was not because my fingers
no longer fit between his
like a perfect zipper;
they did.

it is because now it is someone else's time
to learn all of his favourite things
love his idiosyncrasies
bring out the parts of him
that I couldn't
it is someone else's turn
to lace their fingers through his.

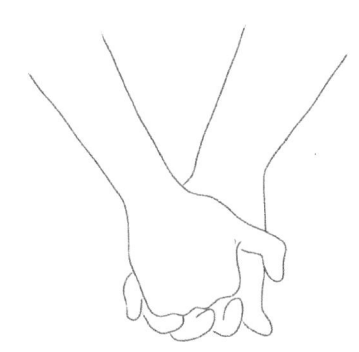

how beautiful is it that
I am still finding doors to open in this city
to places that I otherwise
did not know existed
falling into other worlds
colouring the corners
of an expanding map
that used to be just a grid
a hidden rustic coffee shop
I fell into one morning to read
a marble ballroom with chandeliers
where bankers used to swarm
a bakery on a street
I've walked many times
but somehow never noticed before
maybe there are still doors within me
waiting to be opened
maybe there is always more to explore

— filters

I wish I could give you my eyes
to see yourself with
so you could see
how beautiful you really are
through the eyes of someone
who hasn't been trained
to think otherwise
please
don't let insecurity
blur the beauty
you were born with

clarice goetz

up past my bedtime
waiting on a reply
thoughts spinning cobwebs
throwing out good feelings
insecurity seeping
god, you make me feel disposable

heart strings

how much of the world
am I missing out on
when I'm scrolling through vanity
double tap for digital love
swipe up for capitalism
look up
everyone is looking down
suddenly I feel lonely
my eyes are fogged
how much time have I lost

    — **screened in**

clarice goetz

and I remember
the day you told me
that you noticed
how there was at least one bulb out
in every light fixture in that house

broken appliances
overgrown lawn
you saw the brokenness
in fatherless jobs
that were now left undone

and I remember
the first time you called it
unhealthy
when I didn't want to leave my room
how I used to hide in my closet
because it felt safer

how you met me at my locker
each morning
before we ever walked hand in hand
to make sure I wasn't still settling
for that boy who dragged me by that wrist
accepting what I thought I deserved

do you think that I forgot
in the mess of heartbreak
the way you tried to save me
how you wished for a happier home for me
how you let me borrow your parents
when I felt like a spare child

do you think that I forgot
what you did for me

you kept my head above water
until I could swim myself to shore

heart strings

you have sunk ships
that you probably didn't even know were sailing
because my compass will somehow
always point back to you

clarice goetz

you like the idea of what we could be
like the potential that paint chips have
to colour walls
you just want to distract yourself
from the grey starter paint around you
but you don't really love the colour of me

heart strings

can we really call it
a conversation
if neither of us is listening?

we have nothing in common,
you and I,
except that our lips
seem to like the taste of
each other's skin

clarice goetz

you swing in and out
pretending to care
feigning feelings
that I know are not there
when you get bored
I'm suddenly your muse
but you've never read
a single word I've written,
have you?

    — **not my biggest fan**

heart strings

please remind me
to never shrink myself
to fit inside the lines
that someone else drew
please don't let me forget
to scribble in crayon
every now and then
I need someone
who is not afraid of colour

clarice goetz

I was enchanted by him
he said I was too good to be true
my magic had to be an illusion
that he couldn't see through

but behind the curtain
he found no charade
I fed him no lies
no tricks of the trade

doesn't take much to vanish these days
he was a kaleidoscope of tragic
and for his final act
he disappeared

heart strings

— unwanted advances

tired of the same cheap passes
I'm worth more than an easy message
they're trying to buy something I'm not selling
someone told me to stop answering
why do I feel like I owe them an explanation
I'm done with sparing feelings
before anyone else
I belong to myself

clarice goetz

I want to cut off my hair
ink my skin
I want to dress more like me
than I've ever been
I want the changes I feel inside
to be visible
intentional
I want the growth I can trace in my poems
to look like it's on purpose
I want you to feel
like you don't know me anymore
because you don't

heart strings

sometimes I think it would be nice
to be lukewarm
but I am either hot or cold
I will either lash out, all leather
or soothe you, white lace
it is love
or it is hate
but there is no
carefree in-between with me
I wish I could be anything
but "all or nothing"
this polarity,
it has cost me greatly

clarice goetz

where did you get your sweater?
it's such a nice colour on you
who gave you your smile?
I've never seen a smile so radiant
or a mind so fierce with wit
hands so eager to help
a heart so pure
and wholesome
thank you, on behalf of the world
for your electric laugh
I wish I could hear it more often

heart strings

look for love in tea flavours
or in your new favourite book
because much like your keys
or your wallet when you've lost them,
love will be in the last place you look

clarice goetz

every time I start again
with someone new
I find myself simplifying my essence
to appear more attractive
push my voice up an octave
wear a facade of easy and breezy
smile when I don't want to
rehearse
"easy to love"

but I am not made of lightness
I am heavy
like velvet
I have stopped resisting
the raspy voice
that found me in my 20's
and growls from my chest
my heart is dipped in paint,
I feel things "too deeply"
I used to hate these things about myself,
now I choose to lean into them instead
if you cannot hold the weight of me,
then don't

— words I will give to my daughter

I wish someone had told me this
so I will tell you now
you will be underestimated
your voice will be drowned out

you will be trained to apologize
for things that aren't on you
you will feel like shrinking yourself
instead of taking up space that you're entitled to

you will be shamed
for things that boys are praised for
being a girl is not easy
but there are many things to adore

I will raise you to lead, sweet girl
there is delight in proving them wrong
you will have so much to say
you are your mother's daughter after all

clarice goetz

this is space
I hated it at first
I hated the freedom
I never saw it as a chance
to answer all the questions
I had never asked myself before
I despised the free time
I saw it as 'alone'
instead of
'all mine'
this is
space
that only I can fill

heart strings

there is a roar in me
that some can provoke.
there is a fight being fought
by my sisters.
it is wider and deeper
than I have ever known.
I am often told by good men,
"just don't let it bother you"
they mean well but they will never understand.
how many times I've been followed home.
how many times I've been objectified by men
before they even knew my name.
how many times I've been shamed,
for things that men are praised for.
I am done being patient.
I am done being understanding.
I am done.
I will not calm down.
if you do not see these slights,
then you are not paying attention.
when you ask me why I let it bother me,
my only reply is,
"how *doesn't* it bother you?"

clarice goetz

— thaw

I think I let the winter
make me cold
I became harder on myself
froze out people
to be on my own
maybe the spring will thaw me
maybe I can grow

— **false spring**

I am learning
that I am just like false spring
the fresh air convinced me
that it was here to stay
and then overnight
my healing was blown away
by flurries
and snowstorms
I watched from my pillowcase

the storms aren't a setback,
they're merely part of the process
you were brave to feel them,
it doesn't take away from your progress

it takes time
to heal
it takes patience
to bloom
I keep promising myself
spring is coming soon

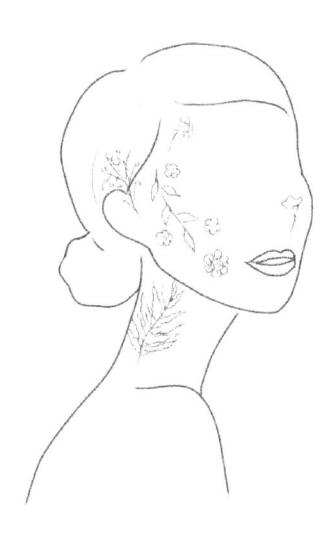

clarice goetz

— **collecting**

it's exciting
finding pieces of yourself
in someone else
when the conversation doesn't stall
but makes a name for itself
I have all of our pieces
like a collection of handpicked shells
and when the tide came
my fingers softened
like wilting stems

heart strings

             I see something in you
                that I can't explain,
                not even to myself.

— **april showers**

'it's time'
the skies told me
I think they told you too
that the years will scatter us
like dandelion seeds
but it doesn't always have to feel this blue
there are other hearts out there waiting
to love someone like me and you
and some days the clouds
might mourn for us
but you know what they say
about april showers,
don't you?

heart strings

> even now, in spite of everything
> one of the most beautiful things
> to ever happen to me
> was when your eyes became
> my favourite colour

clarice goetz

— glimpses

he was always peering in
hoping to see more
he'd ask to see the photographs I took
or the words that I wrote
but I keep these things to myself
like a child running free
unaware of danger
he ran straight for me
I tried to warn him
but he would not take heed
he wanted more than I could give
now there's so much
he will never see

heart strings

> long after I have left your mind
> I will still be beating myself up
> for the things I could not give you
> staring contests with my ceiling
> while I war with myself over it
>
> long after your feelings have dissolved
> and you've forgotten the first flutters
> I will still be retracing my steps
> backspacing messages
> how could I have done this
>
> long after you've discarded me
> as just a crush that got shoved
> I will still be reassuring myself
> that you'll have another to love

I would have disappointed you anyway.

clarice goetz

tell them to run
the other way - fast
I'm a dead end street
my heart is still in pieces
and they'll only get cut on me

tell them to run
to save themselves
from the glass on their feet
apparently we all love to dance
with what won't set us free

tell them to run
to take their lines
their flirt and their smiles
and go use them
somewhere worthwhile

tell them to run
before they've idealized
what we could be
I have nothing to give them
but a sad story

— nourishment

what if I had stayed
in that small town
the one I used to think was big
driving around the same old streets
instead of rushing past subway stations
what if I never traded
power lines
for skyscrapers
practicality
for pipe dreams
is there another me out there somewhere
still sitting by that river
she must be starving
I think the city feeds me
even when I'm not hungry

clarice goetz

— may flowers

april brought things that I didn't expect
cold fingers, warmed by yours
first kisses under tangled umbrellas
secrets kept behind locked doors
learning how you take your coffee
under earl grey skies
swaying on a rooftop
where we watched the city twinkle in our eyes
it's all so new
even though I've been here before
warmer weather is coming soon
and I want so much more
we have both felt the rain
braved heavy storms
we have earned all of the flowers
that may will bring forth

lily of the valley

heart strings

></>
I haven't felt butterflies
like these ones
before
I would recognize
the wings I once knew
almost anywhere
but these ones are a different colour
there are new patterns to memorize
you are something completely new
thank you for the fluttering

clarice goetz

— **overwrite**

even as I move forward
let myself feel new things
I fear that you have too
our history was a chapter for you
a stepping stone
to something better
I felt your heart falling away
tectonic shift
from miles away
I've got new stories now
that you'll never hear
and you've got songs
that remind you of other people

— mother's day

we talked about how florists must be
the happiest
today and on valentine's day
we didn't talk about how
those days have been
the loneliest for us
I can't ignore the flowers
reaching for me
begging me to reconcile
I think about the bruises
she left on my skin
the kind of marks
that a parent should never leave
on their child
I try to empty out my pockets
unpack all of the shame
and guilt I have carried in them
for the years of silence
and soon I am up to my knees
in disappointment
and the sky opens up
to rain with me

clarice goetz

we flutter here
in this liminal place
bated breath
new lines to retrace
there's something kind
in your eyes
it calms the worry
in my mind
we talk about family
the people we've loved
in the past
for the first time
I don't worry
about how long it will last

— meeting point

bright blue eyes
it's all new to me
breath of fresh air
you're just like me
no need to shrink
I can feel fully
please be patient
wait for me
I'm picking up pieces
from another's time
I will meet you there
where the stars
kiss the sky

tulips, variegated

clarice goetz

— wall of words

every poem I write
pushes you farther away
I am building a wall of words
stretching
the distance between us
farther and farther
I know that you must hate the words
I wonder if you check them
I secretly hope you do

oh just to sit across from you
in some doesn't-matter-which cafe
to melt in your hands again
to have your eyes reassure me
that it's okay I wrote them
would you understand
that I'm not angry
that I've forgiven all that you've done
have you forgiven me
for the hell I put you through
have you written off our love
like I seem to have
written
off
our love

have you?

if I could erase the words, would I?
is it too late?
would I trade the poetry for you?
I think that maybe I would.
that's why you are so dangerous
you make me want to give up
on things that I love
when I know you'd probably give up
on me again anyway.

heart strings

— oragami

when I stand in the mirror and see
an origami shape that I don't recognize
I can start to unfold the pieces
for which I once apologized
when I look inside my chest
to find that all the butterflies have died
I can always kiss their wings
and thank them for ever being alive
I'm taking back the things I shelved
in the name of quiet compromise
I am prepared to sweep up
whatever collapses in the meantime
I can always come back
no matter what else falls away
I can always find myself again
here on this page

the moment

I've rehearsed the moment.
the one you wait a lifetime for.
but mine changed
without me noticing
it used to be a man on one knee
asking for me and only me.
my dreams have changed since then;
there are endless roles
to breathe myself through,
books to write,
plane tickets to buy,
photographs that need me.
kind of freeing isn't it?
realizing that the moments
I've been waiting for
are now waiting on me.

heart strings

I want to see beautiful places and feel beautiful things. I want to be heard and seen and appreciated even just by one person. I want to make art and make waves and make love and take chances and maybe even take someone's name. I want to have the words placed on my tongue like sweet little sugar cubes by someone and feel it melt over years and years. I want to feel for the first time, that all the crooked parts of me are a perfect fit for someone else. I want to breathe the air of new places and fall into pockets of the world that are furnished with history. I want friends and polaroids and tacky themed parties with echoing laughs that follow me to my pillow. I want to catch eyes across the room, but not like in a cheesy movie, when the popular guy from school notices the adorkable girl. I want my person. I want that knowing glance, months, even years in. completely undetected by our friends. but it exists for us and in the fabric of our life together. and at the end of it all when we thread all of those beautiful, messy memories together, we are wrapped in a tapestry, telling stories.

clarice goetz

I have learned that this city only has two seasons:
winter and construction.
my heart has been under construction for some time now.
it's not an easy thing to admit
that I have been slowly rebuilding
since you blew up everything we built.
everything I thought I knew, left with you.
I have been taking detours all winter
to avoid this place.
but my good days have started to outnumber my bad days
so I'm picking up my tools again
summer seems like a good time
to start building something new

always remember this:
you don't have to stay
the same person that you've been
you don't owe your past self
any state of permanence
I left her
between the pages of the book
I wrote to heal her
I left the jaded remarks
the broken heart
and unhealed scars
buried deep in the earth
I'll walk forth from this place
as a better version of me
capable of being so much more
than what I thought I could be

    — **catharsis**

Acknowledgments

thank you to my family who have encouraged me throughout the long process of publishing this book. thank you for loving me at my best and at my worst.

thank you to my friends; you have been steadfast in your belief in me. thank you for reminding me of what I am capable of, even when I doubt myself. thank you for pouring all of your light into my life. you know who you are.

thank you to Hilary, my incredible photographer, who has been photographing me for so many years. thank you for being such a wonderful mentor to me and so many others. you always capture the essence of me; you see me wherever I am in my growth and meet me there with your lens. I can only hope to do the same for others with poetry.

thank you to all of the hands that pushed me and lifted me to reach this milestone. there are so many people who have positively influenced me on my creative journey so far. whether our interaction lasted one day, a few weeks, or for many years, the impact was lasting. I have so much gratitude for the web of people who have shaped me into the artist I am.

thank you to my muses, especially C. whether the work you inspired was melancholy or joyous, you changed my life in a beautiful way and I would be completely different if it weren't for you. I will always be grateful to you.

thank you to every single person who has ever shared or liked or even simply read one of my poems on the internet. you inspired me to take my notebooks from some of the darkest times of my young life, and turn them into something that people can use to help themselves heal. and that is pretty magical. keep dreaming with me.

bellflower

ABOUT THE AUTHOR

Clarice is a Canadian writer and actor, raised in Waterloo, Ontario. Growing up with a vibrant imagination and a creative spark in her fingertips, poetry has always been a friend to her. When she isn't dreaming up poems or working on camera, she enjoys being a hobbyist photographer, binge-watching her favourite sit-coms and indulging her obsession with popcorn. Clarice currenty resides in Toronto.

Made in the USA
Monee, IL
22 November 2020